LATE NIGHT SCREWING AND BANGING
A BEDTIME STORY

by Mark Downie

Illustrated by Way Jackson

ISBN: 978-1539316671

First Edition

For my sweet, innocent children.

It is music to my ears every time
you ask to hear late night screwing and banging.

-M.D.

For my... ya. Ditto.
- W.J.

I was deep in a dream,
Asleep in my room.

When I heard a noise come,
Through the walls with a boom.

I sat up with a start,
And didn't know what to do.

I listened in silence,
Hoping for some new clue.

I could see a crack of light,
Shining under the door.

Then I heard some laughter,
Coming from the first floor.

I tiptoed out of my room,
And into the hall.
I was clutching my bear,
Whose name is Rue Paul.

We paused for a moment,
At the top of the stair.
"I hear mommy and daddy."
I whispered to bear.

"Oh how I love those melons!"
I heard my dad say.
"Hands off" said mommy,
"None of that please today."

My dad is a fan of melons,
This is very true.
Of all shapes and sizes;
Cantaloupe, water, or honey dew.

"Wow, they feel even firmer
Than they did yesterday."
Replied my dear dad,
In a most earnest way.

A firm melon as you know,
Means it's not quite ripe.
So daddy would have to wait.
No melons tonight.

"Would you like a taste of my sausage?"
Dad asked with a playful tone.
"Oh, I'd never turn that down."
Laughed mommy with a groan.

I snuck down a few steps,
Not making a peep.
All this talk of food,
There was no way I could sleep.

Then I froze when I heard
My mom yelp "Ooo, that's so hot!"
It must have been Italian sausage,
Mommy likes those a lot.

But they quickly moved on,
They soon forgot about food.
It seemed a delivery had come,
By postman or courier dude.

"That is such a big package!"
My mom said with joy.
"But we must keep it quiet,
So we don't wake the boy."

What did they have
In such a large container?

Staying up to hear more
Was definitely a no-brainer.

I saw daddy walk by,
Then quickly return,
With his tool in his hand,
And a look very stern.

Then there was screwing and banging,
And banging and screwing.
They were making lots of noise,
I didn't know what they were doing.

My dad had wood,
That much I could clearly see.
He was swinging it around,
With a look of pure glee.

Was he making a table,
Or maybe a shelf?
Was it designed by a store,
Or something he dreamt up himself?

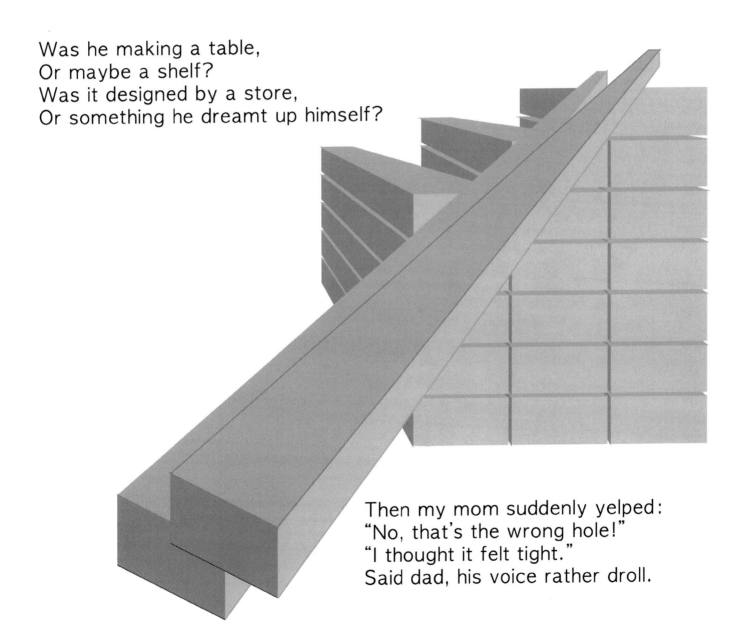

Then my mom suddenly yelped:
"No, that's the wrong hole!"
"I thought it felt tight."
Said dad, his voice rather droll.

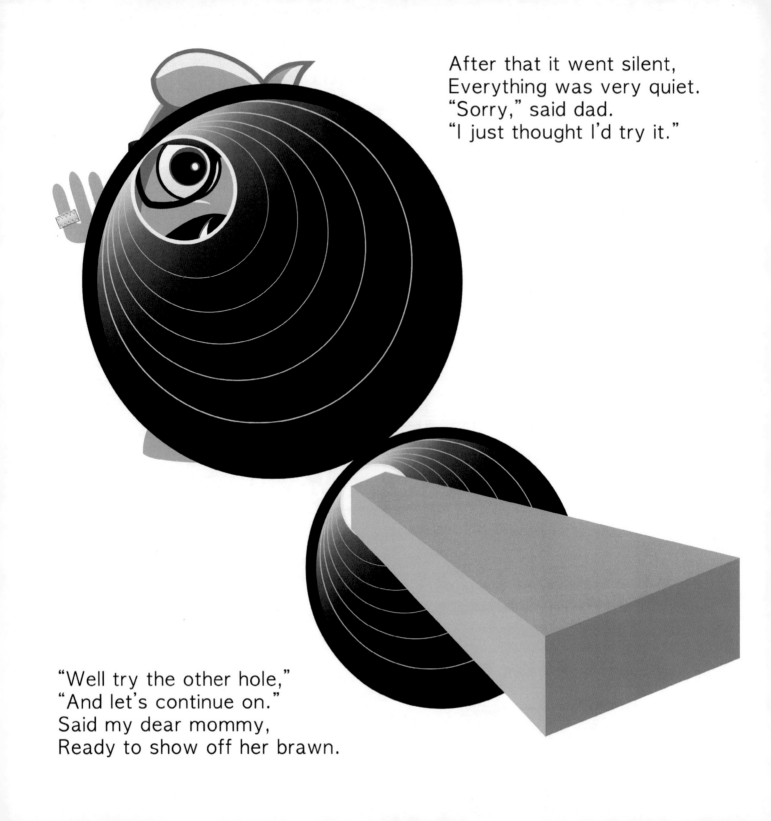

After that it went silent,
Everything was very quiet.
"Sorry," said dad.
"I just thought I'd try it."

"Well try the other hole,"
"And let's continue on."
Said my dear mommy,
Ready to show off her brawn.

I was starting to fade,
More tired than ever!
But I really wanted to see
The fruits of their late night endeavor

Mommy sounded tired too.
"Can you finish off on your own?"
She asked of my dad
With an exhausted groan.

My dad replied without pause,
In a tone kind of prickly:
"If you can just work on the balls,
We'll be done really quickly."

"Sounds like a plan!
I love these big balls."
Echoed mommy's voice,
Through the stairwell walls.

A table doesn't have balls,
And neither does a shelf.
"What is this thing?"
I quietly asked myself.

Daddy kept on banging
As time slowly crept by.
Mommy was humming away,
Then I got a twitch in my eye.

I was so tired,
And it was so late.
I stumbled back to my bed,
I could hardly see straight.

As I pulled up the sheet,
And started to doze,
I kept trying to listen,
Even with my eyes closed.

"You're amazing!" dad said,
To which mommy replied:
"Were we quiet enough,
Or should we have done it outside?"

Then I drifted off to sleep,
With pleasant dreams flowing.
Until the sun rose up,
Telling me to get going.

I got up in the morning,
And had a tinkle.
Then made my bed great,
There wasn't even a wrinkle.

First I stretched really big,
Then put on some socks.
And I went downstairs,
To see what came out of that box.

I turned the corner,
Into the kitchen I went.
To see what had come
From that late night event.

What they had done
Totally blew my mind!
It was so big and grand,
The right words were hard to find.

There was a slide and a climber,
A telescope, and a swing.
A ham radio, a teeter totter,
And a bell I could ring

A marble track ran
From high to low.
And music was playing
From a hifi stereo.

Our kitchen table was gone,
Replaced by air hockey instead.
But the best part of all,
Was up above my head.

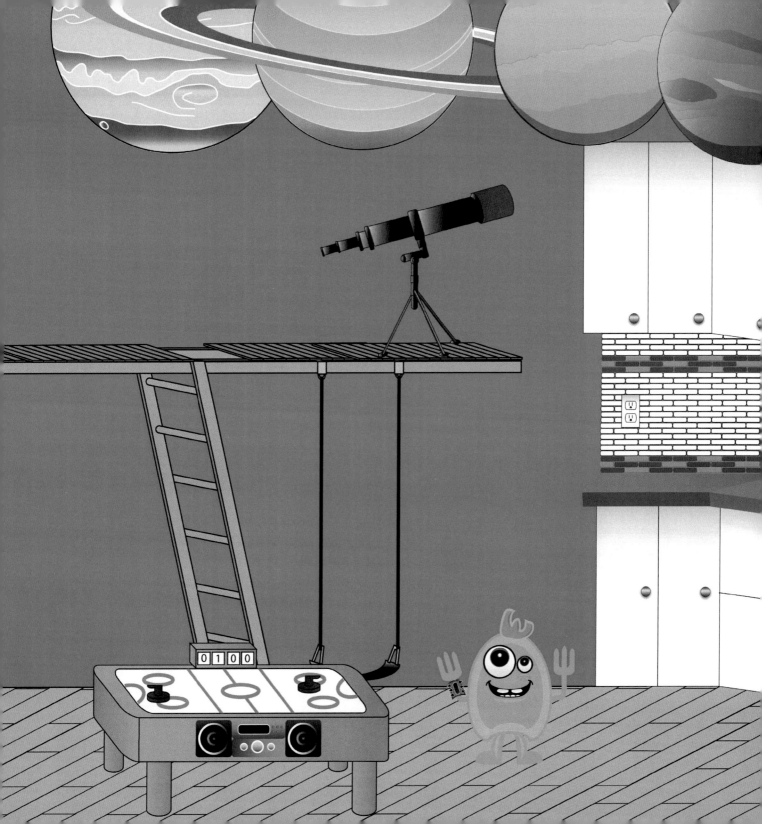

Far far up above it,
Hung 8 balls in the air.
They were vibrantly colored,
Giving it all a sense of flare.

The balls were the planets,
From mercury to Neptune.
Our whole solar system,
Minus the sun and the moon.
(and Pluto of course because that's just a dwarf planet).

"What do you think?" asked Dad,
"We built it just for you.
It was shipped over from Sweden,
It's called a fürgulgërmåku."

"I love it all so much.
I hardly know where to start.
Dad, Uranus is lovely
I think that is the best part."

Mom and dad exchanged a glance,
And I saw them both giggle.

Then out of the blue,
Dad gave his bum a little wiggle.

That was weird.

Then we sat down to enjoy
A breakfast of melon that was ripe.
It was a sweet and juicy cantaloupe.
Daddy's favorite type.

The rest of the day was spent
Playing on the fürgulger-whatever
Because I think you'll agree...

We have the best kitchen ever!

THE END

Made in the USA
Las Vegas, NV
17 January 2024

84481169R00021